CONTENTS

INTRODUCTION

Choose plants that like the setting, treat them well, and there is no need for shady parts of the garden to be dull and depressing. In fact, such sites can be far more interesting than an open sunny area, for many beautiful plants grow best when sited in at least partial shade.

F.B.S.

PLANTS
FOR SHADE

ELISABETH ARTER

HarperCollins*Publishers*

Products mentioned in this book

Benlate* + 'Activex' 2	contains	benomyl
ICI Slug Pellets	contains	metaldehyde
'Keriroot'	contains	NAA + captan
'Nimrod'-T	contains	bupirimate/pirimicarb
'Rapid'	contains	pirimicarb
'Sybol'	contains	pirimiphos-methyl

Products marked thus 'Sybol' are trade marks of Imperial Chemical Industries plc
Benlate* is a registered trade mark of Du Pont's
Read the label before you buy; use pesticides safely

Editors Maggie Daykin, Joey Chapter
Designer Chris Walker
Production Controller Craig Chubb
Picture research Moira McIlroy

First published 1990 by
HarperCollins Publishers

This edition published 1992

© Marshall Cavendish Limited 1990, 1992

A CIP catalogue record for this book is available from the British Library.

Photoset by Litho Link Ltd., Welshpool, Powys, Wales
Printed and bound in Hong Kong by Dai Nippon Printing Company

Front cover: Shady border by Garden Picture Library
Back cover: Alchemilla mollis, ferns and hostas by John Glover

Much of the beauty in a shady garden comes from contrasts of light and dark. The varied tones of green leaves can also be contrasted with light stone paving, walls or plant tubs. Walls painted white will give a sense of space and lighten a gloomy area. Variegated foliage patterned in gold, white or silver suits a dull spot too, but choose well for some of these plants revert to plain green leaves away from bright light or as new spring foliage matures.

Colour contrasts A cool tranquil haven of greenery for relaxing on hot summer days can be created by clever grouping of plants with foliage in different shapes, textures and tones. While many plants flower for only a few short weeks, their leaves may go on looking good for month after month, and sometimes all year round.

Bright red, orange and gold flowers are suited to open sunny plots, but white, pale yellow, lavender and pink show up and look far better set among massed foliage in shade.

Damp or dry Many shade-loving plants prefer moisture-retentive soil and if you have, or are able to create, a damp boggy area you can grow the most luxurious foliage and marsh flowers such as *Iris laevigata,* trollius and candelabra primulas.

Under trees or at the foot of a high wall the earth is often dry and calls for some special preparation for planting. It also needs care afterwards to make sure roots do not dry out too much and the choice of plants should be restricted to those happy in dry shade. The choice will also be more limited in dense shade than in places where a light canopy of overhead leaves allows dappled sunlight to filter through, or where the sun shines for at least part of the day.

Wild flowers With so much interest in conservation these days many people are giving over parts of their gardens to wild flowers and a shaded area can make a lovely woodland glade filled with some of the plants that are native to our British forests and roadside coppices.

LEFT Pale pink pelargoniums are ideal plants for patio containers and provide a splash of colour in a shady patio.

RIGHT *Rhododendron* 'Baden Baden' is another good choice for patio containers.

BELOW Variegated *Euonymus fortunei* and *Hedera canariensis* 'Variegata' bring light to a shady wall and pleasingly frame the tree beyond.

Incentives Soil will not be a problem if your shaded area is limited to a back yard or the space at the bottom of basement steps and everything must be grown in containers. You will be free to choose a compost appropriate to the plants you want to grow. And you can have every bit as good a display as if you lived on the sunny side of the street where there is trouble with hot sun baking and drying out the compost in window boxes and hanging baskets.

Gardening in shade may be more of a challenge than in a sunny open place, but results can be quite as good and give even more pleasure and satisfaction because a bit more thought has been needed in order to achieve that success.

TYPES OF SHADE

Shade in a garden may vary greatly from one part to another. Its extent will change with the seasons as day length alters and the sun rises higher or lower in the sky. There are climatic differences, too, from one area of the country to another, with some plants that grow happily in full sun in the cooler, wetter north doing better in some shade in the drier, warmer south-east.

The situation also changes with the passing of time, as trees grow and spread their branches wider so that a border lightly shaded one summer may a few years later be completely overshadowed when a full canopy of foliage has developed.

There are few places, however, where the sun does not shine for part of the day or where it is not possible to let in some more light. In fact, it is far simpler and quicker to do this than to create an area suitable for shade-loving plants in a completely open garden.

There you may have to wait several years for trees or shrubs to grow large enough to give shade, but in a few hours you can remove some of the lower boughs and thin out those near the top of a tree, or reduce the height and width of a tall hedge.

Dappled shade Under deciduous trees and larger shrubs this type of shade makes a perfect setting for primroses and many of the other woodland plants that bloom early in the year. Many winter and spring-flowering bulbs will be happy if allowed to naturalize themselves here, too. Among these are our native windflower *(Anemone nemorosa)* with white flowers often tinged with pink and *Anemone apennina,* from Southern Europe, that is usually blue.

The lily-of-the-valley *(Convallaria majalis)* will provide a carpet of ground-covering green leaves, and

Creamy white and green variegated hostas, planted at intervals down a narrow border shaded by a high wall. Their pleasing shapes and light colouring show up well against the grey brick of the path and complement their companion plants.

bell-shaped, richly-scented white flowers are produced in May.

The turk's cap *(Lilium martagon)* with its swept-back petals is an easy summer-flowering lily to grow informally among shrubs.

The Granny's Bonnet columbine, lady's mantle *(Alchemilla mollis)* with a froth of acid yellow flowers and the delicate pink or white flowered *Astrantia major* are among many cottage garden plants that thrive in light shade.

Dappled shade under tall deciduous trees and a lime-free soil makes the perfect setting for rhododendrons with big beautiful spring blooms that may be spoilt by frost in an open position and camellias with their showy early blooms and polished evergreen foliage.

Heavy shade Few plants will flower well in summer in the very heavy shade found under wide-spreading trees with thick canopies of leaves. But you can have a good show by choosing some of the ivies, ferns and other foliage plants that will flourish in such conditions.

Select them for contrasting forms, leaf shapes and different shades of green and include some with variegated foliage, such as the green, silver and white ivy, *Hedera canariensis* 'Variegata'.

Colour can be added, too, by growing clipped box, the miniature bamboos, and other plants in terracotta pots, and by using red brick for paths and low walls. The area can be further lightened by painting walls white or using natural stone for paving and tubs.

Dry shade The choice of plants is restricted, too, in shady areas where soil is dry due to rain being kept off by high walls and hedges or the overhead canopy of foliage; the hungry roots of trees add to the dryness by taking available moisture from the ground.

Ferns will have much less luxuriant fronds here than in a damp place, but many of them will thrive in very dry spots.

Too invasive for choice borders, *Lamium galeobdolon* will cover the ground with a carpet of green and

Light shade is best for *Alchemilla mollis*, with its light green leaves and froth of acid-yellow flowers from June to August. A justly popular border plant usually seen spilling over a path or lawn edge, but here effectively complemented by a wooden support.

The delicate flowers of a candelabra primula offset by luxuriant ferns, and both flourishing in a shady, moist spot.

silver leaves on any dry dark site.

Most forms of ivies will flourish also, and generally you will find that evergreen shrubs and other tough woody subjects are a better choice than plants with soft growth.

Moist shade Many moisture-loving plants thrive in shade and looking at those that grow in the wild around a pond will give you an idea of the species to grow in damp dull patches of garden. Here you can enjoy the candelabra primulas, kingcups, globe flowers, several species of iris and other flowering plants that will positively revel in a damp spot. Grow, too, the most luxuriant ferns and foliage plants.

If you have no damp place, you could make a boggy area by digging out and lining a piece of ground as for a pool, but refilling with a mix of soil, peat and garden compost over a drainage layer of gravel. This looks best by a pool, but that should not be sited near trees whose falling leaves would become a considerable problem in the water in autumn.

A shady wall Don't despair because sun-loving climbers will not grow and flower well on a north- or east-facing wall, for many lovely plants will enjoy this cooler position.

Clematis montana will give a mass of white or pink spring flowers here and, among large-flowered hybrids for summer, one of the best is the white *C.m.* 'Marie Boisselot'. Though roses are not shade-lovers, pale-pink and fragrant 'New Dawn' and cream-white 'Alberic Barbier' are two lovely climbers suitable for growing on a north wall.

Virginia creepers *(Parthenocissus)*, that colour so well before the leaves fall in autumn, will thrive here. So will many varieties of evergreen ivy and the deciduous climbing *Hydrangea petiolaris* with its attractive white lacecap blooms, freely produced in summer.

The yellow-flowered, deciduous

Jasminum nudiflorum; the grey-catkined, evergreen *Garrya elliptica* and berried, evergreen *Pyracantha* 'Orange Glow' will give winter colour.

North-facing border So long as a north-facing border is not over-shadowed by high trees and is sheltered from strong winds it will make a good home for many fine perennials, from the pulmonarias and doronicums right at the start of the season through to Japanese anemones and varieties of *Sedum spectabile* that give colour into autumn.

Shrubs, foliage plants and bulbs suitable for other shady sites will flourish here and, among annuals for summer bedding and containers, the modern F_1 Hybrid busy lizzies are really superb.

ABOVE *Sedum spectabile* 'Autumn Joy' and the low-growing *S. lidakense* teamed with silver-grey *Stachys lanata*, which shares with them a dislike of cold, exposed spots and strong winds.

RIGHT Profusely flowering *Clematis montana* 'Rubens' will happily cover a north- or east-facing wall with its small, pale pink flowers.

THROUGH THE YEAR

Even in the shadiest parts of a garden, it is possible to have a variety of plants that will guarantee interest – of flower, foliage or form – all year round. All it takes is a little careful preplanning of what will be happiest in each location before you begin planting.

WINTER

A shady border can look lovely very early in the New Year because many plants of the wood floor flower well before deciduous trees come into leaf. You can grow here some real beauties that revel in a cool root run and humus-rich soil and would not be nearly as happy if they were sited in an open sunny position.

Stars among them are the hellebores whose blooms last for several months. Best-known is the Christmas rose *(Helleborus niger)* with waxen white blooms that are often pictured on greeting cards. However, a much better garden plant is the Lenten rose *(H. orientalis)* that opens in January or February and has big saucers of pink, plum, white or green blooms. *H. atrorubens* is similar, with plum-red flowers that open in December far more reliably than those of the Christmas rose.

A short-lived perennial that will seed around in shady places, our native *H. foetidus* has dark-green divided leaves that contrast well with clusters of nodding, maroon-rimmed, light-green flowers.

A large shrub that prefers lime-free moisture-retentive soil, the Chinese witch hazel *(Hamamelis mollis)* opens sweetly-scented, spidery, yellow blooms very early in the New Year on bare twigs. They show up to best effect against a background of evergreens. This could be a hedge of the common yew *(Taxus baccata)*, the hybrid holly *Ilex* × *altaclarensis*, or the fast-growing, small-leaved

Lonicera nitida all of which can be relied upon to grow well in shade.

Specially good among evergreen shrubs for winter flowers are *Mahonia japonica* with richly-scented lemon racemes against very handsome pinnate foliage, and *Viburnum tinus* with oval dark leaves and flat heads of tiny white flowers that are pink-tinged in the compact form, 'Eve Price'.

A low-growing evergreen shrub that must be planted in groups of both sexes to give good crops of fruit, *Viburnum davidii* has glossy dark leaves and bright turquoise berries.

Under trees or in a gloomy town garden, skimmias are super dwarf shrubs with oval evergreen leaves and in good female forms, such as 'Foremanii', red fruits that last well. You need a male for pollination and the variety 'Rubella' has very showy crimson flower buds.

Many shrubs have more than one season of colour and you can grow *Cornus alba* 'Elegantissima' for its red winter stems and the white and green summer leaves. Both are at their best when the shrub is pruned to the ground in early spring and the soil is moist.

Around these shrubs mass small, early-flowering bulbs that can be left to spread until they carpet the earth with their welcome colour from late January on.

Plant both single and double forms of snowdrop *(Galanthus nivalis)*, winter aconite *(Eranthis hyemalis)*, hardy little *Cyclamen coum* and *Crocus tomasinianus* which bears slim lavender blooms several weeks before the large Dutch type.

SPRING

Could anything be more the epitome of spring than massed primroses growing in dappled shade under trees and shrubs? Grow here the wild *Primula vulgaris* and some of the many hybrid forms that often come into bloom before winter is past. Polyanthus enjoy the same cool fertile conditions and are suited to more formal bedding with double daisies, pansies and hyacinths, too.

Daffodils of all kinds grow well in grass, under deciduous trees, or in a shady bed beneath a wall where they mix well with ferns whose new fronds will come up to mask the dying bulb foliage and give a very effective summer display.

Ideally choose damp grass if you want to naturalize the *Fritillaria meleagris* that is now rare in the wild and has pretty mauve or white speckled blooms. Its handsome cousin, the crown imperial *(F. imperialis)*, is a cottage garden plant with stiff stems topped by bunches of orange or lemon flowers.

Our own English bluebell *(Scilla nutans)* and the larger-flowered blue, pink or white Spanish bluebell *(S. hispanica)* are two more spring bulbs for a shady site.

Tiny bright blue flowers of the perennial forget-me-not *(Brunnera macrophylla)* are followed by big heart-shaped, matt-green leaves that make good summer ground cover.

The pulmonarias also follow early

Naturalized in grass, the dainty *Fritillaria meleagris*, with mauve and white speckled blooms, revels in a damp spot. This delightful flower is becoming increasingly rare in the wild, so it is all the more welcome in spring gardens.

The deep pink, narrow, heart-shaped flowers of *Dicentra eximia*, complemented by ferny blue-green leaves, are another good choice for the shady, spring garden.

bloom with showy summer leaves that are prettily blotched with white in *P. saccharata* that has varieties with red, blue or white flowers. *P. angustifolia* 'Munstead Blue' has slimmer leaves of plain green.

An old-fashioned perennial for good soil and part shade, the bleeding heart plant *(Dicentra spectabilis)* has arching stems of bright pink and white heart-shaped locket flowers and there is a pure white form, too. *D. eximia* has ferny blue-green leaves and is more compact.

The spurges *(Euphorbias)* will grow in most soils and most positions and their showy yellow-green flowers last for weeks. *E. polychroma* makes a neat mound that's good for the front of a border, *E. wallichii* has long narrow leaves with white midribs and *E. wulfennii* makes a bush of blue-green foliage that lasts all year and is topped by large heads of spring bloom.

The flowering currant *(Ribes sanguineum)* is an easy deciduous shrub that will thrive in light shade. The evergreen *Mahonia aquifolium* will grow well in a really gloomy place or a windy corner. Its glossy dark leaves back dense clusters of bright yellow flowers at daffodil time.

The spurge laurel *(Daphne laureola)* with glossy evergreen leaves and scented yellow-green spring flowers is a bushy native that grows well under trees.

Start the biennial honesty *(Lunaria annua)* from seed for branching stems of mauve or white bloom followed by silvery, moon-shaped seed cases. It will then self-sow to come up year after year among shrubs and can be relied upon to lighten any dull corners.

SUMMER

Easy-going biennials also provide good summer colour in shady parts of the garden, and one of the best is the foxglove *(Digitalis purpurea)* and its Excelsior Hybrid form with blooms in a range of pretty, soft colours. They are fine among shrubs or in a dull border. The very tall branching teasel *(Dipsacus fullonum)* attracts many butterflies to its lavender summer blooms and later

Long, cream-white spumes of flowers are borne in July by *Aruncus sylvester*, a plant that revels in fertile damp soil in part shade.

provides showy brown seed heads to feed the wild birds as well as giving winter interest.

The bellflowers *(Campanulas)* supply a lot of good plants for shady places, from the biennial Canterbury bells that give one season of early bloom then die, to the perennial *C. persicifolia* with tall slender stems of white or blue midsummer bloom, and the neat rounded *C. carpatica* with open saucers of blue or white on the rockery, or at the front of a border, at the same time.

With big mopheads of scented bloom, phlox loves a fertile damp soil in part shade and so does the sweet bergamot *(Monarda didyma)* with whorls of red, pink, purple or white flowers and aromatic leaves. Astilbes, with ferny foliage and plumes of summer bloom, thrive here too and so will the goat's beard *(Aruncus sylvester)* that is taller, and larger, with cream flowers.

If soil is good and damp, the rounded evergreen leaves of the bergenias will be bigger and better than in other places, but there won't be many of the showy spring blooms.

Contrast them and the Hostas, whose leaves are often boldly variegated, with long lacy fronds of the lady fern *(Athyrium filix-femina)* and ostrich feather fern *(Matteuccia struthiopteris)* that like good moist soils, or the male fern *(Dryopteris filix-mas)* and soft shield fern *(Polystichum setiferum)*, that will grow in dry places. The hart's-tongue fern *(Phyllitis scolopendrium)* will grow in dense shade on any soil but the strap-like fronds will grow far larger if it is situated in damp, fertile land.

On well-drained soil many fuchsias are hardy enough to leave out all year if you surround the base of the plants with bark chippings or peat in late autumn. Others can be over-wintered inside, before planting out in tubs or borders in late May for several months of colour.

Shade is deepest of all in high summer and then it is good to have a cool, leafy retreat of green foliage plants, with perhaps a few tubs of fuchsias and busy lizzies, or some pot-grown lilies for colour. Among the easier lilies to grow among shrubs in a border is *Lilium amabile*, with turk's cap blooms of bright red, and *L. henryi* with orange-yellow blooms on stately stems of up to 2m (6ft) in height.

Mophead hydrangeas are good summer pot plants for shade, especially in colder areas where they might be frosted if left out all year. The lacecaps, such as 'Blue Wave', and the more compact red 'Geoffrey Chadbund', whose colour does not appear to be affected by different soils, are good shrubs for livening up dull borders.

AUTUMN

Japanese anemones with big saucers of pink and white bloom on tall stiff stems are one of the joys of a shady border from late summer until well into autumn. They look lovely with *Aster ericoides*, one of the few Michaelmas daisies happy in shade. An erect bushy plant with tiny pink or white starry flowers, this blooms into October. So does the rosy-mauve obedient plant, *Physostegia virginiana* 'Vivid'. With erect stems of tubular bloom, it is happiest in light shade on soil that does not dry out in hot weather.

Grow *Arum italicum* 'Pictum' both for the spikes of bright orange fruit and the large, spotted leaves that come later in autumn and go on for months. This contrasts well with our native, evergreen, *Iris foetidissima*, a perennial found in the wild in woodland on dry chalky soil. It has decorative seed capsules that burst open to display showy orange-red seeds in autumn.

A small native tree that grows in quite deep shade on similar soils, the spindle *(Euonymus europaeus)* is best in the variety 'Red Cascade', which has big, bright pink fruits that split to reveal scarlet seeds.

The snowberry *(Symphoricarpus)* will grow in dense shade under trees, but produces far more of the marble-like fruits where the sun

Spectacular is the only word to describe the towering silvery plumes of *Cortaderia selloana*. Striking enough in their own right, they seem even more so by contrast with the rich autumn colours of deciduous plantings close by.

Amelanchier lamarckii is much valued for its wonderful autumnal tones – and it is equally attractive in spring when it bears white blossom and coppery young foliage.

shines for part of the day. The upright 'White Hedge' and pink-berried, arching 'Mother of Pearl' are two good forms.

With flat fishbone-style branches, *Cotoneaster horizontalis* is easy to grow against a north wall or on a shady bank for red autumn leaves that match bright fruits soon taken by the birds. Grow with it the winter jasmine *(Jasminum nudiflorum)* which sports its cheerful yellow flowers on bare green twigs.

Often grown as a houseplant, *Fatsia japonica* might not be a wise choice for growing in the open in colder areas, but thrives in shade in more sheltered parts of the country and does well in town gardens. The large and very shiny palmate leaves make a good backing for rounded heads of milky-white autumn bloom.

Stately pampas grass *(Cortaderia selloana)* makes splendid clumps with big plumes of silver blooms that show up wonderfully well in autumn near Virginia creeper *(Parthenocissus quinquefolia)* and some evergreen shrubs. This very popular climbing plant is often planted against walls, but looks splendid too when growing up through an old tree, over the roof of a shed, or on a netting fence.

The snowy mespilus *(Amelanchier lamarckii)* is one of those valuable shrubs with more than one season of beauty. In April, white blossom blends with coppery young leaves, and in autumn these turn to brilliant tones before falling.

The snowball bush *(Viburnum opulus 'Sterile')* provides round balls of white May bloom and good autumn leaf colour, but *Viburnum opulus* itself has lacecap flat heads with true flowers that are followed by jewel-like red fruit in autumn.

SOILS FOR PLANTING

When planting in shade it is important to bear in mind the quality of the soil, which kind of shade you're dealing with, and the particular site – whether close by a wall or under trees, for example. Immediate aftercare is also crucial, but that does not mean that it is very demanding.

LEFT Shade-loving dwarf rhododendrons flourish in peaty soil, and are available in a good range of colours.

RIGHT There will be no problems about keeping the peat moist in this site by a pool, where more rhododendrons and other acid-loving plants grow side by side.

BELOW RIGHT A crowded shrub border takes a heavy toll of soil nutrients, so add a good general fertilizer each year.

Soils Soil in shady parts of the garden is often dry and hungry because trees, shrubs and hedges keep off rain, particularly in summer when leaves are fully out, and their roots take up a lot of the available plant nutrients. Places shaded by high walls are also protected from rain and tend to have poor, hungry soil, because they do not benefit from the humus that comes from fallen leaves and what roots there are have to compete for limited moisture.

Digging in heavy applications of 'Forest Bark' Ground and Composted Bark, well-rotted manure, garden or spent mushroom compost at a rate of one or two large bucketsful to the m^2 (sq yd) will help improve both moisture retention and the nutrient level of the ground. A 5-8cm (2-3in) thick layer of similar material spread on the ground around established plants in autumn will help build up a friable top layer of soil, and improve moisture retention and nutrient levels.

A handful per m^2 (sq yd) of a general fertilizer such as Growmore lightly forked into the topsoil before planting, or on established borders in spring, is also beneficial.

Soil can be improved, too, by adding generous amounts of leafmould made by stacking for at least a year fallen leaves collected from other parts of the garden, and this is specially good for those plants that like woodland conditions.

Peat is sterile and so does not add plant foods to the soil, but applied generously it much improves moisture retention and the structure of both very heavy and very light land. Where soil is alkaline copious peat dug in or as a top dressing will also make it easier to grow well plants that prefer acid conditions.

You can make beds entirely from peat when you are growing dwarf

rhododendrons and other shade- and acid-loving plants such as camellias or pieris. However, if you live in an area where mains water is alkaline there may be difficulty in finding enough soft water to keep the peat moist all summer.

Another way of growing lime-haters in an area where the soil is chalky is to plant them in tubs filled with an ericaceous compost.

Choose a special seed mixture of drought-tolerant grasses for a lawn in a shady place, be prepared to feed the turf more than usual and never cut too low. Where shade is very dense under large spreading trees it is wiser to put in low-spreading ground cover plants rather than attempt to make a lawn.

Planting Whether container-grown or bare-rooted, all plants benefit from being stood in water for several hours before a move and if this has been done those in pots will usually come out with their root ball intact and the roots undisturbed.

Where soil is dry and hungry take

extra trouble over making planting holes. Each one should be taken out several times larger than the ball of soil and compost around the new plant. When you are preparing to plant among trees or near a hedge you often have to cut through some smaller roots in order to take out a hole. This can be done with sharp spade or secateurs.

However, it is obviously wise to move the site to one side if you meet any major roots and to avoid putting in one thing too near another. For example, a honeysuckle or other climber that is intended to grow up through an old tree is better planted 1m (3ft) or so to one side.

For a shrub or large plant fork a bucketful of 'Forest Bark' Ground and Composted Bark, rotted manure or other organic matter into the subsoil at the bottom of the planting hole, or for a smaller plant add a spadeful of the same material.

Next, knock in any stake that may be necessary for supporting a taller

specimen, fill the planting hole brimful with water and allow this to soak into the ground all around. Add a peat-based proprietary planting mixture, a spadeful for a large plant

ABOVE AND LEFT
When replacing plants in a well-filled border, it is often necessary to cut through some roots of neighbouring plants while taking out a hole. If you use a sharp spade or secateurs, established plants should come to no harm. The main consideration is that the newcomers should be suited to your kind of soil.

and a trowelful for a small one, around the inside of the hole.

Lift the plant in carefully with root ball unbroken, or with the roots spread out well over the area of the hole if it is bare-rooted. On poor soils use some earth from the vegetable plot or other more fertile part of the garden to help refill planting holes or, if that is not available, old potting compost.

Once the hole has been filled in firm the soil around the plant with your boot or shoe so that it will not be loosened by wind or frost, then surround it with a 5cm (2in) thick mulch of 'Forest Bark' Chipped Bark or well rotted organic matter to conserve moisture.

Watering is vital during the next few weeks, particularly in the drier, warmer months. To make sure that water sinks in around the new plant rather than running off the soil surface make a hollow with your heel at one side, or sink a small flower pot in the ground so that it performs the service of a funnel.

Foliage on conifers and broad-leaved evergreens tends to dry out in warm weather before a plant has time to make new roots, and spraying overhead with water every few days in the month after planting helps avoid this.

Frost protection If you are going to fill containers with summer annuals remember that frost-tender subjects such as busy lizzies and *Begonia semperflorens* cannot safely be stood outside until late May. However, you can prepare containers a few weeks earlier and keep them inside or in a sheltered place, covered at night until plants are established and it is safe to leave them outside all the time.

This is a particularly good plan with hanging baskets and tubs that will be stood in draughty places where wind might damage young newly-planted annuals.

To protect conifers from drying out in warm weather, mulch the ground and spray overhead with water as necessary. This is particularly important (indeed, crucial) for new plantings.

AFTERCARE

Once planting has been completed the amount of aftercare depends almost entirely on your style of gardening. A shady area with trees and shrubs underplanted with naturalized bulbs and biennials, wild flowers and ground cover plants will need very little attention. A town courtyard filled with seasonal plants growing in containers will need daily care though, due to its small size, this may not take up much time.

Once shade-loving plants such as hostas, ferns and rheums are properly established, they need minimal attention. But they cannot be left entirely to their own resources if you want them to continue to give a good display.

Feeding Even in the informal woodland garden you will need to feed plants on a regular basis, for tree and shrub roots take a lot of nutrients from the soil. One of the best ways of doing this is by putting down annual top dressings of garden compost in February/March, before new growth commences. Collect fallen leaves, disease-free garden rubbish, lawn mowings (unless weedkiller has been recently applied) and kitchen waste for the compost heap, adding some animal manure or some proprietary activator in order to hasten the rotting down process.

Fallen leaves can be collected, made into a heap on their own and allowed to rot down into leafmould for top-dressing around those plants whose natural home would be in woodland soil. Spent mushroom compost, spent hops, well-rotted stable or farmyard manures are other bulky organics that are suitable to use for top-dressing.

If none of these is available, feed with an inorganic general fertilizer such as Growmore. Apply this at the start of the growing season, scattering a handful to every m² (sq yd) in among the plants. Some additional feeding through the growing season can be provided by use of a proprietary liquid feed such as ICI Liquid Growmore.

Liquid feeding at least once every two weeks will help ensure strong, healthy plants and a long season of colour in summer containers. Although they will not dry out as rapidly in a shady place as in full sun, you will probably need to water hanging baskets and other smaller containers every day in hot weather. Watch for signs of drying out in all shady borders in summer and water them accordingly.

Mulching Generous use of mulches will help conserve moisture, keep down weeds and when organic materials are used will help feed the soil and improve its structure.

Top dressings of compost and manures will form mulches if they are not forked in. Fallen leaves can be collected and spread several centimetres (inches) deep around shrubs. In a small area bark chippings or peat do the job well and either one will give an attractive finish to beds and big containers.

When hand-weeding, make sure you remove all of the roots.

Inorganic general fertilizers are applied by hand, sparingly.

Compression sprayers are good for general use.

A special dispenser ensures the correct measure of liquid feeds.

A hoe can make weeding larger areas easier on the back.

Mulching round plants not only conserves moisture, it keeps down weeds.

Cultivation Little, if any, surface cultivation should be attempted in areas planted with naturalized small bulbs that could be accidentally dug out and thrown away with weeds. Nor should it be necessary once ground cover plants have become established and are doing their job efficiently.

To avoid risk of the soil becoming compacted in these areas walk on it as little as possible and never in wet weather. Compaction can be a real problem in shady borders on heavier soils. It can be reduced by not walking on the ground when it is wet and by mulching to reduce the need for digging and hoeing.

Lightly fork over the soil between plants to break up the crust and let in air before putting down the mulch. You may need to do this again in autumn during routine tidying before the top growth of some herbaceous plants has died down and made them invisible until spring. In between times a trowel is a very good tool for slicing off young weeds and aerating the soil surface.

Phlox and many other longer-lived border plants should be lifted every three or four years, split up and just a few pieces of the strongest young growth from the outside of each clump replanted.

Pruning Cutting back plants is necessary for a number of reasons. They may be growing into less vigorous subjects, taking light from windows or obstructing paths or there may be dead or frost-damaged wood to come out. Better, bigger flowers or brighter foliage and bark may be carried on young shoots, or you may want to clip plants for hedges or formal shapes.

Clip vigorous ground cover plants regularly with the shears for neater more compact growth and to prevent them from spreading too freely. Prune rose of sharon *(Hypericum*

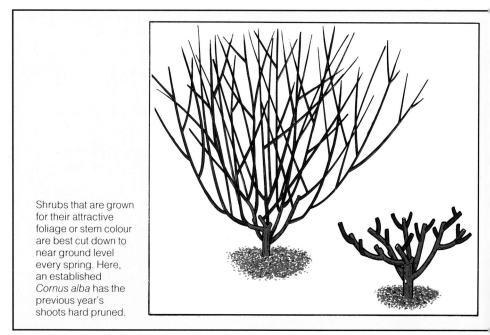

Shrubs that are grown for their attractive foliage or stem colour are best cut down to near ground level every spring. Here, an established *Cornus alba* has the previous year's shoots hard pruned.

ABOVE *Lonicera nitida* makes a good hedge for shade if its small, neat foliage is clipped several times during every growing season to keep it in trim and encourage dense growth.

RIGHT Once a hedge has reached the required height it becomes an easier matter to keep it trimmed to the ideal profile: wedge-shaped, widening at the base.

calycinum) in early March and yellow archangel *(Lamium galeobdolon)* after flowering in late spring.

Removing some spent blooms before seeds ripen will prevent honesty, columbines and other biennials and short-lived perennials self-seeding too freely.

Winter Jasmine, flowering currant and other shrubs that flower on shoots produced in the previous growing season should be pruned soon after flowering.

Cornus alba and other shrubs grown for foliage and stem colour are best cut down to near ground level early every spring. Fuchsias that have been left in the open garden all winter should be cut low every April even when frost has not killed the top growth.

Little pruning is normally needed for evergreen shrubs, but where dead, diseased or frost-damaged material needs removing or they must be reduced in size, late April is the best time to cut. Spent flowers should be removed from rhododendrons as soon as they have faded.

A *Lonicera nitida* hedge will need clipping several times during every growing season and will stand severe pruning if it is overgrown. A single cut in August is usually sufficient for established box and yew hedges or for clipped specimens.

Even in window boxes and hanging baskets a little discreet pruning is often necessary before the end of summer to prevent the variegated ground ivy *(Glechoma hederacea)*, ivies, or strong-growing fuchsias and other vigorous plants swamping those of more modest habit.

PROPAGATION

Most shrubs and many perennials last for years and so there is seldom need to raise new plants. Bulbs, too, will usually also go on and on, often multiplying considerably if allowed to grow naturally. But, with annuals and other short-lived plants new material is frequently needed and you can save a considerable amount of money and gain great satisfaction from home propagation.

LEFT For spring or summer displays, sow seeds of pansies in gentle heat in February or March.

RIGHT *Aquilegia vulgaris* will obligingly self-seed if allowed to grow informally.

Half-hardy annuals Few annual flowers grow well in shade and those that do need care to start them successfully. Some people find busy lizzies hard to germinate and prefer to buy in tiny rooted plantlets from the seed firms to grow on to flowering size. But it is not hard to propagate them at home if seed is sown in small pots of vermiculite at the end of winter and these are stood in a heated windowsill propagator until tiny seedlings appear.

Pots can then be placed on the windowsill in a warm room until the seed leaves have fully expanded. The seedlings can then be pricked out into small individual pots or plant starts (consisting of a block of nine tiny plastic pots) filled with a peat-based potting compost. When they have developed sufficiently for roots to show through the bottom of these first containers they should be moved on to 6-8cm (2½-3in) individual pots and grown on in a frost-free greenhouse or indoors until flower buds show.

Harden off by gradually introducing to cooler conditions before planting outside after frost risk is past. Poor results come from planting out in open ground when too small or before the end of May.

Fibrous-rooted begonias need similar treatment, but are slower-growing so they should be sown by the middle of February. The monkey flower (Mimulus) is not so tender and though raised in much the same way from a March sowing does not need much warmth after pricking out and should grow on successfully in a cold greenhouse.

Though truly perennial, pansies are best treated as annuals. For late spring and summer displays sow in gentle heat in February or March, pricking out and growing on as for the half-hardies, but with no need of warmth from the pricking out stage, and planting outside as soon as plants are large enough.

For the winter and early spring

show, sow under cold glass in small pots around midsummer's day and prick out into small individual pots for growing on in a cold frame with the cover removed, or direct into a cool fertile part of the garden at 10cm (4in) apart each way, to grow on into strong plants. The best winter display comes from pansies planted before the end of September.

Biennials and short-lived perennials Foxgloves, Welsh poppies, honesty, columbines and teasels are among these short-term plants that are very generous with seed. If allowed to grow informally with no dead-heading or hoeing and over-zealous weeding nearby they will provide you with ample self-sown seedlings to maintain a supply for year after year.

Start off the first season's plants by sowing in shallow drills in a

A cold frame is indispensable for the hardening off of young plants. It need not be a very grand construction: a simple box shape topped with a sheet of glass that can be adjusted to let in more air as required will suffice. But a more permanent frame is a worth while investment.

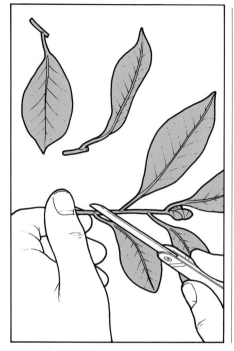

LEFT Camellias can be propagated successfully from leaf bud cuttings, consisting of a single leaf attached to a short section of stem.

BELOW Use a dibber to make holes in the compost and insert the stems. Firm in. The cuttings will need a basal temperature of 18°C (64°F).

Plants such as polyanthus can easily be propagated by division. Select an over-large clump and, holding it by the roots in both hands, carefully pull and tease the roots apart. Then replant. When dividing a plant that has established a tough crown, insert two back to back garden forks at the centre of the plant and lever apart.

seedbed on well-drained soil in the open garden in May or June. Thin seedlings or prick out into a nursery bed on fertile soil in a partly shaded place at 10-15cm (4-6in) apart each way to make sturdy plants for moving to their flowering positions in autumn. A bit of the vegetable plot shaded by runner beans or tall peas is an ideal site. Canterbury bells and double daisies are raised in the same way, but they will need sowing anew each year.

Polyanthus, drumstick primulas, the candelabra primulas, primroses, the peach-leaved bellflowers and sweet bergamot are among perennials that are better raised from seed sown under cover. Seedlings are then pricked out into a nursery bed as soon as they are large enough to handle.

Sow in small pots filled with a peat-based seed compost such as 'Kericompost', with a very thin covering of the same material, in March or April. Stand the pans in a part-shaded cold frame and make sure the compost does not dry out. If you do not have a frame the pots can be stood on a tray in a cool place in the garden with a sheet of glass balanced on top.

As an alternative to the nursery bed you can prick out into individual 8cm (3in) pots filled with potting compost and sink these to half their depth in a cool border to grow on until ready to plant. This works well when only a few of one kind is needed and avoids root disturbance at planting time.

Quite a lot of other perennials can be raised in this way, but because improved named varieties seldom come true from seed it is more usual to propagate by division of the roots.

Fuchsias 'Mrs Popple' and 'Tom Thumb' are among the so-called 'hardy' fuchsias that normally come through winter safely in the open, but whether you want to increase stock of them or to keep the more tender varieties going from one year to another it is easy to raise new plants from cuttings.

These can be taken in late summer and over-wintered under glass in a frost-free place, or taken in spring from new shoots growing up from the base of old plants. Each

Pricking out *Rudbeckia* seedlings.

cutting should ideally be 5-8cm (2-3in) long, cut off from the tip of a sturdy young shoot just below a leaf joint. All but the top pair of leaves should be removed and about six cuttings inserted around the sides of a small flower pot filled with damp perlite. You can first dip the cut ends into hormone rooting powder such as 'Keriroot'.

Stand the pot in a warm, part-shaded place, and make sure that the perlite does not dry out. New growth from the top will tell you that a cutting has rooted and is ready to be potted individually.

Quite a lot of shrubs can be propagated in a similar manner, cuttings of half-ripe young shoots taken in July or August usually rooting quite well in a cold frame.

PLANT PROBLEMS

With so many different types of plant growing in shade there could be a great many different pests and diseases. But well-grown plants should be healthy enough to resist disease and recover quickly from pest attacks. So, there should be little need to resort to chemical remedies. The following are the most likely problems you will need to deal with.

PESTS

Aphids (Blackfly, Greenfly) Colonies collect on young shoots and leaves, mostly in early summer. Rub them off with thumb and fingers, wash off with a powerful jet of water or spray with 'Sybol' or 'Rapid'.

Birds They peck flowers, especially the early primroses and polyanthus. Surround plants with black thread stretched between a few short canes.

Froghoppers Masses of whitish froth known as 'cuckoo spit' on many different kinds of plant in May and June indicates the presence of infant froghoppers. The damage is seldom serious; 'spit' looks unsightly but can be washed off with a powerful jet of water from a hose.

Slugs They eat irregular holes in leaves and leave silver slime trails, a particular problem with hostas and tender young seedlings. Surrounding plants with bark chippings will help keep the pests away. Where a large number of slugs are causing damage, place a few ICI Slug Pellets around the base of the plant and replace them at regular intervals – particularly during wet weather.

DISEASES

Black sooty film seen on leaves of plants growing under sycamore, lime and some others trees is caused

Never let a colony of aphids become this well established.

Characteristic honey-coloured toadstools of the deadly honey fungus.

by a fungus forming on the sticky secretion from aphids feeding on the trees. The only cure is to spray the trees with a product such as 'Rapid' or 'Sybol', but this can be difficult with large specimens – spray as much of the lower foliage as possible.

Honey fungus Shrubs and trees, or major parts of them, may suddenly die. The fungus produces clusters of honey-coloured toadstools above the ground, whitish mycellium beneath the bark, and dark bootlace growths along the roots. Cut down, dig out and burn infected wood, and seek professional advice on how to prevent spread of the disease. Do not replace trees or shrubs on the same site for a few years.

Mildew This waxy white powdery coating on leaves and young shoots should be sprayed with Benlate plus 'Activex' 2 or 'Nimrod'-T.

SOIL AND GROWING TROUBLES

Alkaline soil Can cause yellowing of leaves between the veins, especially on young foliage of acid-loving plants. Heavy dressings of peat will help, or apply Sequestrene chelated compound.

Dry soil If it is very dry flower buds may fail to develop properly, and growth be stunted and withered. Water the ground thoroughly and regularly throughout dry weather.

Damping off Seedlings flop over and die, usually due to too little light and air. Sowing thinly and uncovering as soon as seed leaves appear should avoid further trouble.

Poor germination of seedlings is usually due to using old seeds, too little moisture, covering seeds too deeply, or too low a temperature.

SIXTY OF THE BEST

Whatever the size of your plot and whatever your style of gardening there are shade-loving plants to suit your needs. The following have been chosen not only because they are willing to grow in dull north-facing positions or gloomy beds under trees, but also because they are good garden plants.

BULBS

Anemone nemerosa
The wood anemone carpets the ground under deciduous trees in many copses in early spring with pretty, deeply lobed leaves and white flowers that are often pinkish on the undersides. It will grow on any but very acid soils.

Cyclamen hederifolium
Pink or white elfin flowers of this small cousin of the popular pot plant open from August to November. Ivy-like dark-green leaves marbled with silver come up in September, and last through to May. Left alone, this will self-seed on a north-facing rockery. *C. coum* has more rounded flowers early in the New Year.

Eranthis hyemalis
The winter aconite opens buttercup-like flowers backed by toby-dog ruffs of green before January is past in most years. It moves best straight after flowering, while the leaves are still green, and left undisturbed will spread to form a big colony.

Galanthus nivalis
The common snowdrop is another small bulb to move 'in the green' in early spring and allow to increase naturally until it carpets the ground under shrubs and trees. Bell-shaped white flowers with green tips to the inner segments come in both single and double forms.

Leucojum aestivum
The summer snowflake, that actually blooms in March and April, is rather like a giant snowdrop, but all the segments of its green-tipped white bells are the same length. Bright green daffodil-like leaves can be a nuisance in a formal border.

Lilium martagon
The turk's cap lily with petals rolled back like a turban above a cluster of showy anthers is a strong-growing

Pink flowers of the hardy little *Cyclamen hederifolium*

Young foliage and flowers of *Epimedium* × *rubrum*

species that thrives on chalk, needs little attention and grows well among shrubs. Both the light-purple and white forms will grow to 1-1.5m (3-5ft) high.

Narcissus
Most members of the large narcissus genus will grow well in some shade. Varieties can be chosen for flowers from February to late May and range from tiny miniatures for the rockery to trumpet and double daffodils, large and small cupped and multi-flowered narcissi and sweet scented jonquils.

Scilla nutans
The bluebell that carpets woodland in many parts of Britain with deep blue every May is a splendid bulb for naturalizing under trees. It will grow from 20-50cm (8-20in) high, depending on the general condition of the soil.

GROUND COVER

Epimedium × rubrum
This is one of the best of a genus of hardy perennials to grow for pretty, ground-covering foliage. Spikes of dainty, reddish May bloom blend well with the new leaves which, at first, are a deep bronze-pink, then deep green through summer and orange and gold in autumn.

Geranium macrorrhizum
A hardy geranium from Southern Europe, this makes compact bushy plants with five-lobed leaves that

are aromatic when crushed and small magenta-pink flowers from May to July. There are varieties with pale lilac or white flowers and all give superb cover under trees.

Hedera helix 'Hibernica'
No site is too shady for the Irish ivy to grow until it carpets the ground with large, dark evergreen leaves. The closer you plant the more quickly will cover be complete. *H.h.* 'Glacier' has small leaves edged with silver-grey that give equally good cover in a smaller area.

Lysimachia nummularia
The creeping jenny loves a shady site on damp ground, but will grow on dry soil. It will spread to form a carpet of rounded, bright evergreen leaves and small, single, golden flowers in June and July.

Vinca minor
The lesser periwinkle will carpet the ground around the base of a tree or

Vinca minor

Lysimachia nummularia

taller shrub with oval evergreen leaves. There are variegated forms with green and gold or white leaves and in light shade a bonus of blue, purple or white flowers.

FOLIAGE PLANTS

Arum italicum 'Pictum'
The Italian arum, cousin to our native lords and ladies, is much

Arum italicum 'Pictum'

Bergenia cordifolia

larger in every respect. Spikes of bright orange poisonous fruit are showy, but it is grown mainly for the arrow-shaped green leaves, handsomely marbled with white, that appear in autumn and continue to give a good display until June.

Bergenia cordifolia
Elephant ears is a common name given to this easy-going hardy perennial because of the big leathery leaves that shine as though they have been polished. Clusters of very early spring (usually pink) flowers are a bonus in part shade.

Hostas
The plantain lilies are grown more for their very ornamental leaves than for the spikes of summer bloom. Foliage may be green as in 'Krossa Regal', almost blue as in 'Bressingham Blue', handsomely variegated in spring as in *H. fortunei* 'Picta', or all through summer as in 'Gold Standard'.

Iris foetidissima
Though grown by floral arrangers for its split capsules of orange-red seed, the native Gladwyn iris has greatest merit as a foliage plant, specially valuable for dry chalky soils in shade. Clumps of rich-green leaves look good all year and contrast well with lacy fern fronds.

Orange-red seeds of *Iris foetidissima*

Anemone × hybrida, in flower from August to October

Lady fern

The lady fern *(Athyrium filix-femina)* is happy in shade, not fussy about soil and among our most decorative native foliage plants. Grow, too, the soft shield fern *(Polystichum setiferum)* whose old fronds stay greenish through winter before dying down as new ones start to grow up.

FLOWERING PLANTS

Anemone × hybrida

The Japanese anemones, with saucers of pink or white, single or double bloom on tall, slender stems from late summer until well into autumn, take some time to settle into a new site, but once established are hardy perennials that will go on for many years with scarcely any attention.

Aquilegia vulgaris

The columbine in its old Granny's Bonnet form, with tight double May flowers in soft pinks, blues, mauves and purples, and pretty blue-green ferny leaves, is a rather short-lived

Begonia semperflorens 'Superbe Red'

perennial that will seed itself generously in a part-shaded border.

Astilbe × arendsii

There are many varieties of the hybrid astilbes with light feathery plumes of red, pink or white bloom in June to August and ferny leaves, coppery tinted when young. They are hardy perennials for moist soil and are good mixed with candelabra primula and moisture-loving iris.

Begonia semperflorens

There are many F_1 hybrid forms of these colourful, dwarf-branching,

Campanula carpatica

Digitalis Excelsior Hybrids

single, or double in the very popular cultivated form 'Flore Pleno'.

Campanula carpatica
A lovely clump-forming perennial bellflower for the front of a border or rock garden, this has upturned cup-shaped flowers of blue or white from June to August. *C. muralis* can be invasive, but is good for growing over a low wall or big rocks. Its smaller blue-purple bells go on towards autumn.

Convallaria majalis
The lily-of-the-valley with short arching stems of richly-scented white bell flowers amid big mid-green leaves in May is a hardy perennial to grow where it can spread freely. It is a good choice for a bed at the base of a wall or for dappled shade beneath deciduous trees and shrubs.

Dicentra spectabilis
The bleeding heart plant has arching stems of locket-shaped, rosy-red blooms with protruding white inner parts in May and June, and pretty ferny leaves. There is also a pure white variety of this old-fashioned hardy perennial.

Digitalis purpurea
The wild foxglove is a woodland plant that thrives even on dry soils and in quite dense shade. Spikes of rosy-mauve flowers, with pretty spots inside, vary from 90cm (3ft) to 2m (6ft), depending on the soil. A biennial that dies after one flower-ing, but self-seeds quite freely. The Excelsior Hybrid form may flower for two seasons.

Helleborus orientalis
The lenten hellebore is a hardy perennial with big saucers of pink, plum, white or green bloom that

fibrous-rooted begonias that are treated as half-hardy annuals to bloom from early summer to autumn. They are very weather-resistant and grow well in both dull shady places and full sun. 'Cocktail Mixed' includes plants with both green and bronze leaves and a good choice of flower colours.

Caltha palustris
The kingcup, or marsh marigold, is a perennial that loves moist places under trees and is ideal for a natural or contrived boggy area near a pool. Bright golden spring blooms are

stay fresh for many weeks. The leathery, divided, evergreen leaves look tatty when old and are better cut off before flowering.

Impatiens 'Super Elfin'

One of the superb dwarf F_1 hybrid busy lizzies that are best of all half-hardy annuals for summer beds and all kinds of containers in shade. The 'Mother of Pearl' mixture of pastel shades shows up specially well in duller places and blooms continuously from June until the first frosts.

Lunaria annua

Honesty is a biennial with branching stems of bright mauve, or white, scented flowers followed by moon-shaped seed cases, the outer parts peeling off to reveal silvery linings to arrange with dried flowers. The autumn garden display lasts far longer in a north-facing border away from rain and wind.

Lunaria annua (seed cases)

Moisture-loving Mimulus

Meconopsis cambrica

The Welsh poppy, a native of damp rocky places and woods, is a short-lived perennial to allow to seed itself and pop up in unexpected spots. Cheeky yellow or orange flowers are mainly in early summer and usually single, though there are double forms, also in both colours.

Mimulus

The monkey flower is moisture-loving and ideal for growing beside a pool. Its modern compact, vigorous F_1 Hybrid forms such as 'Malibu' are good annuals for edgings, window-boxes and hanging baskets so long as they are not allowed to dry out.

Paeonia officinalis 'Rubra Plena'

The old red cottage peony with big, rounded, double crimson blooms in late spring looks best in a border away from early morning sun that might damage petals covered in late frost. This perennial will go on for

Paeonia officinalis 'Rubra-Plena', an exotic crimson-red hybrid

Meconopsis cambrica

years with little care and has handsome foliage that can be relied upon to look good all summer.

Pansies

Pansies like cool, fertile soil and last longer in part shade than in a sunny bed. There is a big choice of varieties best treated as annuals, some with very large blooms and some with flowers little larger than the wild heartsease. Universal Hybrids are superb for growing in winter beds and containers.

Phlox paniculata
There are many varieties of the phlox with big mopheads of fragrant summer bloom in shades of pink, mauve, crimson and white on erect stems from July to the end of summer. They are perennials for good soil, like plenty of moisture and thrive in light shade.

Polygonatum multiflorum
Solomon's seal is an old plant that needs hardly any care - if grown among shrubs or other perennials in a shady border. Arching stems carry pendant white May flowers and opposite pairs of fresh green leaves that turn yellow in autumn.

Primula vulgaris, a compact dwarf species, flowers in March and April

Primroses, F₁ hybrids

These modern cousins of the wild plant are best treated as annuals, raised from a spring sowing to bed out or fill window-boxes and other containers in October to flower mainly in spring, but often starting in winter. Most have large blooms in bright colours.

Primula vulgaris

The common primrose with pale yellow single flowers amid fresh green leaves will grow on most soils in part shade, but makes plants with larger leaves and blooms in damp soil. The main flowering is in April, but in sheltered places this hardy perennial often blooms before winter is past.

Saxifraga urbium

The London pride makes rosettes of evergreen leaves that give good ground cover in a shady place. The perennial sends up stems of small starry pink flowers in May. A very good form is 'Elliott's Variety'.

SHRUBS AND CLIMBERS

Arundinaria viridistriata

A very hardy bamboo with rich yellow and green variegated leaves and erect purplish canes. It will grow in a tub and is quite small in a shady place, but can reach up to 2m (6ft) high. The foliage is brightest on young canes produced by pruning low in autumn.

Aucuba japonica

Spotted laurels are easy evergreens that thrive on most soils and sites. Male forms such as the boldly marked with gold 'Crotonifolia' and speckled 'Variegata' are most widely planted, but with them the female,

Female plant of *Aucuba japonica*, bearing its scarlet berries

Camellia × *williamsii* 'Donation'

narrow-leaved 'Salicifolia' will produce a host of bright scarlet berries.

Buxus sempervirens
Happy on most soils, the common box can be allowed to grow freely into a tree or big bush, or be clipped to shape for a formal garden. In a town courtyard, box will grow well in tubs. The variety 'Suffruticosa' has medium-sized, glossy green leaves and makes a very good low hedge for edging borders or beds. Plant 13cm (5in) apart.

Camellia × *williamsii* 'Donation'
One of the best of a good group of hybrid camellias, 'Donation' has an upright, almost tree-like, habit and big semi-double, silver-pink flowers over a long period from mid-winter through to May. It likes a site away from morning sun, against a wall or under tall trees.

Euonymus fortunei 'Silver Queen'

Creamy-white and green variegated leaves of this easy-going Japanese evergreen take on a pink tint in winter. New spring leaves are patterned with creamy-yellow. A slow-growing, small shrub of compact habit – about 40cm (16in) high with 1m (3ft) spread – this will however gradually climb to great effect if it is planted against a wall.

Hedera colchica 'Dentata Variegata'

Fuchsia 'Mrs Popple'

With cerise and purple blooms, 'Mrs Popple' is one of the hardiest fuchsias to grow in the open all year on well-drained soil, or to use for containers or bedding through summer. 'Tom Thumb' is a dwarf small enough for a rockery. There are many others to stand out in the warm months and quite a few will even grow all year in drier borders.

Hedera colchica 'Dentata Variegata'

This showy form of the Persian ivy is very hardy and once settled in grows rapidly to cover a wall and spill over the top in a cascade of huge leaves patterned in primrose, silver and green. This ivy also makes good ground cover in shade or can be grown up a pillar.

Hydrangea macrophylla 'Blue Wave'

'Blue Wave' is a splendid lacecap hydrangea for acid soil with flat

Jasminum nudiflorum, the yellow-flowering winter jasmine

Juniperus × *media* 'Pfitzeriana', a wide-spreading shrub

heads of tiny true flowers surrounded by a ring of sterile florets. It makes quite a big bush – about 2m (6ft) high, with 2m (6ft) spread. 'Geoffrey Chadbund' is more compact and a light red.

Hydrangea petiolaris
The climbing hydrangea is a strong-growing, self-clinging species that will cover a high shady wall. At midsummer big heads of white lace-cap bloom made up of tiny true flowers surrounded by a ring of four-petalled sterile ones contrast with the large green leaves.

Jasminum nudiflorum
The winter jasmine is one of the most beautiful and easy-to-grow shrubs that flowers in the dark months. Starry yellow blooms open in milder spells on bare green twigs from November to March. It is good against a north or east wall, or it can be equally striking cascading down a bank.

Juniperus × media 'Pfitzeriana'
Deservedly popular, the pfitzer juniper makes a wide-spreading shrub that gives very effective ground cover with stout branches of grey-green foliage. It will grow well on chalk and makes a lovely foil to the sometimes spectacular autumn leaf colour on deciduous trees.

Lonicera pileata
This dwarf, bushy relative of the honeysuckle is a shade-lover that will grow almost anywhere and makes a hummock of horizontal branches with small, shiny green

leaves that fall in severe winters. It is pretty in the spring when new, brighter leaves appear.

Mahonia aquifolium

The Oregon grape has dense clusters of golden-yellow, scented spring bloom and glossy evergreen leaves whose individual segments look a little like holly. Later there are bunches of very decorative blue-black fruit that earned the shrub its common name. It forms a thicket good for ground cover.

Mahonia japonica

The lily-of-the-valley tree earned its name because of the fragrance of the lemon-yellow flowers that come in whorls on branch ends backed by very handsome, shiny, pinnate ever-green leaves, providing welcome colour from December to March.

Parthenocissus henryana

All self-clinging Virginia creepers are good in dull spots and this Chinese species shows the white markings along the main veins of its

dark-green leaves best when planted against a north or north-west wall. There is also a glorious red autumn leaf colour.

Prunus laurocerasus 'Otto Luyken'

A low, compact variety of the cherry laurel with horizontal habit and erect stems of narrow, shining green leaves. The massed spikes of white flowers open in April and May. It is

Pyracantha 'Orange Glow'.

Parthenocissus henryana (autumn)

Prunus laurocerasus 'Otto Luyken'

Skimmia japonica 'Foremanii'

Viburnum davidii in fruit

happy on most soils and can also be planted successfully under trees.

Pyracantha 'Orange Glow'
Outstanding among the firethorns, 'Orange Glow' makes a vigorous shrub of dense habit, superb against a north or east wall. Evergreen leaves make a perfect backing for clusters of showy white June flowers and the mass of orange-red berries that last through to spring.

Rhododendron 'Elizabeth'
One of the best of many hybrid evergreen rhododendrons for a small garden, Elizabeth will make a bush 60-90cm (2-3ft) high and up to twice this width. Clusters of rich deep-red flowers open in April or May.

Ruscus aculeatus
The butcher's broom is a native suckering shrub that will make a

dense clump of stems of spiny dark evergreen foliage and is tolerant of dense shade on dry soil. When plants of both sexes are grown it produces marble-like red fruits.

Skimmia japonica 'Foremanii'
One of the best female skimmias, this has oval, light-green leathery leaves and creamy-white, scented spring flowers followed by bright red berries which ripen early and last through winter. For good fruiting grow several plants along with the male variety 'Rubella'.

Viburnum davidii
Viburnum davidii is another shrub of low, compact habit that must be planted in groups of both sexes to ensure pollination of the clusters of white midsummer bloom. Bright turquoise-blue berries contrast well with the glossy evergreen leaves.

INDEX AND ACKNOWLEDGEMENTS

Picture credits

John Glover: 4/5, 7(b), 19(b), 20(t), 32/3,42.
S & O Mathews: 6, 9, 10, 11(t), 34, 38(t).
Harry Smith Horticultural Collection: 1, 18, 19(t), 20(b), 21, 22, 35, 36(t,bl), 37(t), 38(b), 43(b), 44(t), 45, 46(t, bl, br).
Michael Warren: 7(t), 8, 11(b), 13, 14, 15, 16, 17, 25, 27, 29, 30, 31, 36(br), 37(b), 39(t,b), 40(b), 41(t,b), 43(t), 44(b), 47(tl, tr).
Rosemary Weller: 26, 40(t).

Artwork by Simon Roulstone

48